Only
One
Life...

1997-98 NWMS READING BOOKS

RESOURCE BOOK FOR THE LEADER

IMAGINE THE POSSIBILITIES
Edited by Beverlee Borbe

FOR THE READER

BY GRACE TRANSFORMED
God at Work in Brazil
By Tim Crutcher

ONLY ONE LIFE . . .
The Autobiography of Lorraine O. Schultz
By Lorraine O. Schultz with C. Ellen Watts

JESUS WILL REPAY
By Becky Hancock

THAILAND: LAND OF THE WHITE ELEPHANT
Edited by Jean R. Knox and Michael P. McCarty

TO THE SHELTER
Journeys of Faith in the Middle East
By Kay Browning

WHERE THE RIVER FLOWS
Bringing Life to West Africa
By Linda Seaman

Only One Life...

The Autobiography of Lorraine O. Schultz

Lorraine O. Schultz
with C. Ellen Watts

Nazarene Publishing House
Kansas City, Missouri

ISBN 083-411-643X

Printed in the
United States of America

Cover design: Paul Franitza

10 9 8 7 6 5 4 3 2 1

CONTENTS

Preface		7
Acknowledgments		9
1.	The Voice of the Master	11
2.	Go West, Young Woman	19
3.	To Africa by Bits and Pieces	29
4.	Yes, Lord, Yes!	35
5.	Tongue-Tangled Teacher	43
6.	Not Just Peanuts	55
7.	Escape at Dawn	65
8.	Safe—but Grounded	75
9.	Dig This Retirement	81
10.	Full Circle	89
Epilogue		94

About the Author

Lorraine O. Schultz was a longtime missionary for the Church of the Nazarene in Mozambique. In her long life, she authored numerous books and magazine articles on missions and archaeology, her two great passions. Lorraine passed away on May 10, 1996.

Preface

When my telephone rang that Friday in January 1996, the caller got right to the point: "This is Lorraine Schultz. I'm writing my autobiography, and now I've had this fall. My deadline is March 15. Can you help me?"

The call came as a surprise. I did not know Lorraine very well and was in fact a little awed by this remarkable woman who had accomplished so much. Still, we made a good team. Lorraine had seven of her early draft chapters carefully organized and typed. I had a word processor and a soft spot in my heart for missionaries.

"You may have to write the last two chapters," Lorraine said. She did the rough draft herself—on a yellow legal pad with her arm in a sling. "I now know where they got the word 'painstaking,'" she said with a characteristic twinkle as she handed me those last rumpled sheets.

On May 10, 1996, Lorraine suffered a stroke following surgery and went to be with her Lord. Then came the rest of the story.

We had made repeated revisions on the manuscript, but still more anecdotes and accolades began to surface. I did my best to incorporate this material and still leave Lorraine's way of telling a story intact wherever possible. While my name may appear on its cover, this book is very much Lorraine's.

—C. Ellen Watts

Acknowledgments

Before she died, Lorraine had three people and one machine she wanted to thank—Irene Craig, her typist for early drafts; Norm Rohrer, friend and writing instructor; and me and my word processor. My list is longer.

First, I am grateful to Lorraine for a paper trail that has made my work easier and to her sister, Jane Scarth, for so graciously sharing letters and scrapbooks, clippings, diaries, and more. Thank you to Pauline Doll Wallace, Pat Buffett Leigh, Marjorie Stockwell, Jane Tustin, Betty Sedat, Charles and Roma Gates, Ina Ashley, Mary Lou Steigleder, and the many other friends and missionary colleagues who took time to share by phone and letter. Thanks also to those whose words I've borrowed to appear in the between-chapter "Glimpses."

—C. Ellen Watts

Glimpses

Lorraine was another no-nonsense African missionary to breathe fervor and evangelistic zeal with intellectual responsibility. She was indeed a great educator. We will miss her. Her students will mourn for her, but heaven rejoices when her works have preceded her.

—Donald D. Owens

Dear Father and Mother,
I am what I am because you folks led us in the right way. I am glad I am your daughter.
Love,
Lorraine

Lorraine at age 3 with her sister Jane.

1

The Voice of the Master

O GOD, PLEASE SPARE MY CHILD!" Mother prayed as she saw my sled veer suddenly to the left.

Moments before, she had pushed me off for a ride down a snowy hillside near our home on Martha's Vineyard, Massachusetts. Halfway down, the sled had struck a chunk of ice hidden beneath new-fallen snow, propelling an unsuspecting five-year-old toward two heavy iron rails that fenced our garden.

The pipes loomed before me. Quickly I lay back on the sled and went flying underneath.

Mother ran down the hill. At the fence, she sat me on the sled and measured. Had I remained upright, the lower rail would have struck me in the face. Holding me close, she exclaimed, "Thank You, God, for protecting my child." Unbeknownst to a little girl who loved sledding, He would one day do so again.

Calling upon God was not new to Ada Schultz, who grew up in Spring Grove and Gettysburg, Pennsylvania, and trained to be a deaconess in a

Methodist school in Washington, D.C. Father farmed near Westtown, New York, and held an exhorter's license in Simpson Methodist Episcopal Church in Jersey City, New Jersey, where he and Mother were married October 10, 1910.

The next year, Father accepted a job with Owen's Poultry Farm, and they moved to Martha's Vineyard, an island just off Cape Cod. Born on the island on April 25, 1915, I enjoyed a happy childhood with my younger sister, Jane, who became my favorite playmate.

Six towns dotted the narrow island that was but five miles wide. We were never far from the ocean or, for that matter, from the dusty odor of chickens. The old saying was true for Father and for us: "The farmer doesn't go to work—he wakes up surrounded by it!"

The 110-acre farm's 8,000 birds produced thousands of hatching eggs, and we moved around the island with Father's work. The house I liked best was on Red Farm. A typical Cape Cod home, it featured wide-plank floors and a narrow stairway leading to the half story beneath its slanted roof. According to local legend, a woman had hidden her cow in its cellar during the Revolutionary War to prevent soldiers from confiscating "Old Bossy" for food.

Martha's Vineyard was once a mission field to the Indians. On Sunday afternoons our family often took a 10-minute walk across a field and into a patch of woods to a mile-square village called Christiantown. My favorite place to explore was a little Indian cemetery near the old chapel, where small fieldstones marked gravesites.

One day Father brought me an Indian arrowhead he had found in the field.

"What is it?" I asked.

Captivated by his simple explanation, I did not know that I had just been introduced to the fascinating world of archaeology. Or that, at six years of age, I would be hooked for life.

Since my father believed that church steps were sure steps toward family happiness, we attended Lambert's Cove Methodist Church. Its wooden benches were old and uncomfortable, and the preacher's sermons long. I learned to watch; when he closed the big pulpit Bible, I knew we would soon be driving home in our shiny Maxwell car for Sunday dinner—almost always chicken, of course.

When I was six years old, my parents enrolled me in the one-room schoolhouse across the road from the church. Then they began to talk of moving, and I was left with little time to complain about the mile-and-a-half walk they said was good exercise for me.

Moving, of course, meant saying good-bye to my new school, Red Farm, and my favorite canine friend, Mr. Owen's little dog, Nipper. Later on, a picture of Nipper listening to his master's voice coming from an old-fashioned phonograph became a trademark for Victor Talking Machine Company (now RCA) that was recognized worldwide. Nipper and I had two things in common, for I would also enjoy world travel and learn to listen for the voice of my Master.

That winter we said farewell to our Eastern relatives and moved by train to Ferris Poultry Farm near Grand Rapids, Michigan. Because no family member had ever ventured beyond Pennsylvania, we called our new location "the Far West."

While we liked living in the more up-to-date house, we now had no car and no way to get to church. The farm manager said he was Nazarene. So were some of the farmhands. They invited us to go in the farm truck to the Church of the Nazarene. Although my parents had never heard of the Nazarenes, they agreed to give the new church a try. Pleased with the church's strong Bible emphasis, they were also glad for Sunday School for Jane and me.

In spite of a 20-mile-per-hour speed limit that made the 10-mile drive seem like a long one, Father began going with some of the men on Sunday nights. One Sunday they took a different route and passed by a Methodist church. Hopping off the truck, he told the others he thought he'd walk back and take a look. A billboard in front of the Methodist church announced a film for the upcoming service. Since films in the church were then frowned on by many, he hastened back to the Church of the Nazarene. His decision marked the beginning of a new life for our family and would soon mean a life-changing experience for me.

As my understanding of God's love began to grow, I noticed the shining faces of people as they came away from the church altar. The Holy Spirit spoke to my heart, and I knew I needed Jesus as my own personal Savior. I was 11 years old when I walked down the aisle of Grand Rapids First Church and prayed until I knew my sins had been forgiven. Peace flooded my heart as I began what was to become a lifelong walk with God.

My parents believed that time spent in *God's* house meant better times in *our* house. So after we bought another car, we attended our own church regularly as well as every tent meeting and revival. Each year, during Father's two-week vacation, we all went the 40 miles to Hopkins to camp meeting. There we enjoyed children's and youth services and heard many of our great Holiness preachers for the first time.

Before age 13, I knew God was calling me to Africa. One afternoon, during one of the missionary services I liked best, all who felt called to serve on a mission field were invited to come forward to the altar. Timidly I walked down the aisle and knelt on the straw-covered floor of that big tabernacle. Pastors and laymen came to pray with us. Looking up through my tears, I recognized Mrs. Charles Cowman, as the tenderhearted author took time to pray for a little girl who very much wanted to be a missionary. Even at that early age, my eyes were fixed on Africa.

Then, sometime during my teens, my toes began a painful downward curling that left my feet permanently crippled. As I struggled to overcome the strange malady, my dream of becoming a missionary at times seemed impossible. But while doctors did not know what had caused my affliction (polio perhaps?), I knew with certainty that God had called me to Africa. Unless He directed otherwise, I would hang on to my plans and get on with preparation.

So I went with Jane to the school near Ferris Farm and practiced piano lessons. When Mother found that a neighbor had studied under a pupil of famous concert pianist Ignacy Jan Paderewski of Poland, she enrolled us in her music classes for the summer. In spite of the Great Depression that hit us especially hard during my high school years, I purchased my own Bible in 1929 with my first earnings. I still have that old Bible with its many verses and passages of Scripture underlined. In spite of my love for reading, a note on its flyleaf reminds me that it took nearly two years for me to read it through the first time.

Ready for my senior year, I found it hard to leave Michigan after a cut in Father's hours forced a change in employment, taking us south to Indiana. Then our bank closed, and my meager savings for college were lost. While the money was later refunded, jobs were hard to find. I walked to the homes of my pupils and taught piano for 10 cents a lesson. Every dime counted. In 1930 it would take 1,500 of them for me to go to college.

Some time after Father's job again ended, he noticed an unusual ad in the *Herald of Holiness.* "Jobs open for two Nazarene farmers," it read. His application accepted, the new position took us back to where we were again near our grandparents and other relatives.

There was also work on the large farm for Jane and me. We worked 10 hours a day that summer for 15 cents an hour. In a five-day week, we could earn as much as $7.50. We were almost rich! I raised the price of piano lessons to 25 cents. By summer's end I had saved $90.00 for college and had tithed faithfully while doing so.

That August I spoke with the president of Eastern Nazarene College (ENC) during camp meeting. When I told him the amount of my savings, he assured me jobs were available on campus to help with further expenses. God had heard my prayers. I left for ENC that September, praising Him for the series of doors He had opened for me. Now that I was finally on my way, I intended to prepare in the best way possible for my future in Africa.

Lorraine at her high school graduation

Glimpses

Dear Diary,

The Lord checked me up this morning about staying up so late the night before and then expecting Him to help me in an examination. Leola removed the callus and massaged my feet. I treated her to ice cream. . . . Another poem published in the Herald of Holiness. *. . . The Lord is wonderfully supplying my every need. Praise His name forever and forevermore!*

Prayer for Holiness

How oft I cried, "Lord, heal my broken spirit,
*   I know I'm Yours, yet battles rage within;*
Temptation, pride, and anger conquer daily,
*   Lord, free me now from all indwelling sin."*
Praise God! Today I found Him in His fullness.
*   My pride, ambition, self, is gone at last;*
My heart has yielded to Him, and this moment,
*   He cleansed my longing soul from all the past.*
It's real! I'm now committed to Him fully,
*   My life, my plan, my all is in His care;*
He sweetly sanctifies my very spirit,
*   And perfect love is mine; He's answered prayer!*
                                            —Lorraine O. Schultz

2

Go West,
Young Woman

IN SEPTEMBER 1934, four years after the Massachusetts Legislature granted permission for the college to award the bachelor of arts degree, college president R. Wayne Gardner welcomed me to Eastern Nazarene College. The college, along with the rest of the country, was still caught in the pinch of the depression.

My first campus job put me in charge of student time slips. Having no time clock, I relied on honest faces and accepted each student's word. In another job, as "chief butter cutter" for ENC's 150 students, I had barely mastered the art of cutting 80 even pats to a pound before depression economics forced the number to 120!

Along with classes taught by godly professors—theology, missions, literature, history of holiness—the Spirit-filled preaching of Pastor E. E. Angell made my heart hungry for more of God.

I had often heard holiness preached and from time to time had sought the blessing of entire sanctification. While I sometimes professed it, the experience never seemed to work for me. Now as I read

J. A. Wood's *Perfect Love*, I knew I did not measure up. Then, near the close of a Wednesday night prayer meeting in Canterbury Chapel, Dr. Angell invited folks to the altar to pray. I hurried forward. Moments later, the blessed Holy Spirit filled my heart with His perfect love, and I knew that the work I had longed for was real!

In 1936 G. B. Williamson became our new college president. Since he was more strict concerning student accounts, I wondered how I would fare. My only dependable cash income was a monthly $10 from my Aunt Edna, which I faithfully turned in at the office. Since the dollar for my tithe to the church had to come from some other means, I accepted any job I could get.

Along with kitchen duties and serving in the dining room, I worked in the home of General Superintendent H. F. Reynolds and sometimes cleaned and cooked or watched children for some of my professors and for others. While all were kind and many became friends, all my hard work did little to put cash in my pocket, pay for orthopedic shoes, or keep me from falling asleep over my studies.

While busy cleaning Canterbury Chapel one Saturday night, I heard sirens. Dropping my dustcloth, I ran to the back door and saw fire and smoke pouring from the roof of Munro Hall, the girls' dormitory where I lived. As I watched, Dr. Williamson, his white shirtsleeves rolled, worked tirelessly alongside the firemen.

"What a president we have!" I thought as I rushed to the rear of the dorm, where a fireman gave me permission to dash into my room long enough to grab a few items. The fire had started in the attic. While upper floors suffered both fire and water damage, the entire first floor, my room and few belongings included, had been spared.

At the end of my first three years, my meager earnings had not kept up with expenses. I still owed money. Would Dr. Williamson allow a student having no funds to enroll even for her senior year? In my heart I still knew the answer. The God who had called me to Africa would see me through.

I knew I must find full-time summer employment. When I learned that one of my professors and his family also needed jobs, I remembered that work could always be found on the farm where my father worked. The manager said he could use extra help, and Father agreed to the plan. With Mother away caring for her aging parents in Pennsylvania, the professor's wife and I were left to do the cooking. When he was not out in meetings, my professor worked alongside his three sons on the farm. At summer's end, in a transaction that took place only on paper, he transferred to my account some of the money the college owed him. For the first time in three years, I was debt-free.

But now someone had told me that only women with nurse's training were being assigned to missionary service. So I wrote to the superintendent of Samaritan Hospital Nursing School in Nampa, Idaho, explaining my plans to enter nurse's training the next year. A return reply suggested I complete my senior year at Northwest Nazarene College (NNC), across the street from the hospital, and on September 1 begin the three years of nursing school at the same time.

That night, after everyone else had gone to bed, I knelt beside a living room chair and reminded my Lord. Other than the monthly $10 from my aunt, I had no money with which to register at ENC, let alone a college where I knew no one. The plastic cards used for VISA and other such credit services had not even been invented yet, and Father earned but $30 a week. How could I possibly pay for a 3,000-mile bus trip?

After laying my case before Him, I stayed on my knees until God drew near. Looking up, I noticed the calendar with its scenic picture from the great Northwest on the opposite wall. Gazing raptly at that picture, I knew God had shown me His answer.

The next morning I wired Samaritan Hospital to say that I could not possibly be in Nampa before September 21. When a telegram came saying the date had been an error, that nursing school would begin on September 21, I asked Father if he could take me to Pennsylvania to say good-bye to Mother and to Jane, who had been with Mother for part of the summer.

Father answered slowly: "Are you sure you're doing the right thing?"

"I've prayed, and God has given His answer," I said. "My only regret is leaving ENC." In Pennsylvania, while Mother seemed a bit unsettled, she did not discourage me.

Soon after I arrived in Pennsylvania, I handed Jane the NNC catalog. A moment later, she showed me a page in the catalog. "Look at this," she said.

"NNC offers the teacher training I can't get at ENC. Maybe I'll join you." This pleased our parents.

A few days later, Jane departed from Philadelphia, while I boarded a bus in Boston. We met in Indiana and continued by bus, arriving in Idaho together.

Founded in 1920 by Dr. and Mrs. Thomas Mangum, Samaritan Hospital provided excellent training for those of us who attended the nursing school, which was added a few years later. I loved the hospital, and my mind hungered toward studies I might find useful in Africa. Along with the class or two that nursing students were allowed to take at NNC each semester, we were privileged to acquaint ourselves with furloughing missionaries who came to the hospital for treatment. What a rich training field!

The first two years passed quickly. Jane completed her education and began teaching. Grandfather died, and our parents moved to Nampa to try out this "Far, Far West" where their only two children had settled.

The year 1940 came. Of the 11 who graduated, several would later head overseas to a variety of mission fields: Bob and Lela Jackson to Argentina and Africa; Geraldine Chappell, my roommate, to India; Ethel Thomas Franklin to India; and I to Africa. Having earned my bachelor of arts degree in biblical literature and theology at NNC and passed my registered nurse's exam for the state of Idaho, I put on my faithful orthopedic shoes the following year and walked across the stage to receive my bachelor of science degree in nursing education.

Then, in 1941, came the word I had waited so long to hear: my appointment to Africa had been made official. I spent awesome days in Kansas City, meeting with the General Board and getting acquainted with Nazarene World Missionary Society officers and furloughing missionaries. General Superintendent R. T. Williams officiated at my ordination during the Idaho-Oregon (now Intermountain) District Assembly in May.

By then World War II was in full swing. Two dates were set for me to sail, and both were canceled. Travel to Africa was out of the question. During those days of uncertainty, I did private duty nursing and ministered through music and to children during district home mission campaigns.

Aware of my call to Africa, yet still willing for me to come if only for a short time, the Lyons, Colorado, Church of the Nazarene near Boulder called me to be their pastor. Later, C. Helen Mooshian, a friend from ENC, joined me as copastor of the Daniels Garden (Edgemont, Colorado) home mission church, where we held services in a portable tabernacle. While there, I purchased a tired jalopy for $50 and promptly dubbed it "Speed." No matter how hard I stepped on the gas, I could never get that car to go anywhere near the speed limit. I later sold "Speed" for $40 and doled out another $125 for "Victory," a more dependable Chevy that got me through the summer.

Recognizing a need for Christ in that town, we agreed that empty pews were an item we could not afford. We called in dozens of homes, inviting all kinds of people to a church where Helen led singing,

I played piano, and we took turns preaching. Within six months our congregation had grown from 25 to 107. We broke the record on Easter Sunday with 136 in Sunday School. By early fall we resigned and handed the newly organized church over to a regular pastor.

Then came the exciting day when that anxiously awaited telegram finally arrived from Kansas City: "CAN YOU BE READY TO LEAVE FOR AFRICA WITHIN A MONTH?"

My answer to C. Warren Jones, my Lord, and my church was "YES!"

Earlier a letter had come from Kansas City explaining that due to limited finances the church must ask newly appointed missionaries to raise their own money for equipment. I had responded to that letter in faith. The God who had seen me through college could surely help with equipment. I began saving some of my Christmas and birthday gifts.

When I arrived back in Nampa to pack for Africa, I opened my chest of love gifts. One by one, needed items had come in. During that last month of packing, friends continued to fill my trunk with beautiful linens, cutlery, dishes, and everything else I could possibly think to need. While "love" contains but four letters, through those generous givers love became mighty big to me.

Nurses Evelyn Fox and Elizabeth Cole were about to leave for their second terms in Swaziland, and I would fly with them. World War II still being in progress, civilian travel across the North Atlantic was prohibited. We would fly to Argentina, board ship there, and sail to South Africa via the South Atlantic.

On a cold November day in 1943, Evelyn and I left Nampa, carrying two suitcases each. An excited crowd of family and well-wishers gathered at the train station to see us off. As I waved farewell to Father and Mother and Jane and her husband, I suddenly realized I had signed a five-year contract!

Then God's peace enveloped me. Fifteen years ago He had called me. I was His ambassador. Now the conductor was calling.

Slowly the train pulled away from the station. We were on our way to Africa.

**Lorraine and Geraldine Chappell,
her Samaritan Hospital roommate.**

Glimpses

Stegi Mission Station

Dear Father and Mother,

Today Miss Lovelace is making me speak to her in Zulu. We study for two or three hours each day after school. I don't hear too much yet, and she will only answer me in Zulu. . . . Saturday I walked a long way into the hills and visited homes with two of the Bible school students. I took along a borrowed guitar, and the Africans loved it. . . . Sunday I gave my first testimony in Zulu. The Africans arranged a circle of flowers around my chair. . . . I preached on the "Highway to Holiness" through an interpreter.

Miss Lovelace has some gasoline lights that petrify me. The only other light I have is a kerosene lamp. Its wick is about finished, and the chimney is badly cracked. They say you can't get any in Africa. We use candles sometimes, but they are rationed. I succeeded in getting flashlight batteries, but they will probably only last three weeks.

What do you suppose I found in my bed? Two of those worm-looking things that grow here, and a little lizard lying nice as you please.

My love to both of you,
Lorraine

3

To Africa by Bits and Pieces

THE STREAMLINER chugged past Idaho's sage-brush, dipped south through the Wasatch Mountains, and rolled on to where Denver First Church of the Nazarene had arranged a farewell service for Saturday morning. Elizabeth Cole arrived from Montana, and our Africa-bound trio continued on to another farewell at Kansas City First Church on Sunday evening. How wonderful everyone was!

When we got to New Orleans, not one of our passports stamped with necessary visas had arrived. But we had to be patient; this was wartime. Two days after our plane had left for Argentina without us, the passports arrived. Two more days passed before we could board another flight.

Since jets had not yet made it to the drawing board, we experienced still more delays—an overnight stop in Costa Rica, a week in the Panama Canal Zone, nights in Peru and in Salta, Argentina. After flying through deep valleys with the Andes Mountains towering perilously close on either side, it was a relief on December 3 to finally touch down on the solid ground of the Buenos Aires airport. Argentina's missionaries were there to greet us.

"How soon do we sail for Africa?" I asked first thing.

Missionary Spurgeon Hendrix shook his head. "Not soon. We've kept in touch, and no immediate sailings for Africa have been set. You may be here for many weeks."

Although none of us spoke Spanish, we soon learned the meaning of *paciencia,* for we heard it repeatedly for the next several months. Meanwhile we helped in whatever ways we could.

One Sunday night Elizabeth and I were invited to fill in at a church pastored by the Hendrixes. Following my sermon and a short time of fellowship, we started for home around 10 P.M. But trams were crowded with people returning after a weekend at the beaches. Not one tram paused near us.

After counting 12 passengers clinging to the outside of a tram, we were about to give up when one stopped. Finding ourselves in "standing and pushing room only," we gladly got off at our transfer corner and hurried to the island. Again we waited. Every tram was loaded. Soon 11:30 P.M. . . . midnight . . . 12:30 A.M. Our host missionaries would be worrying.

I had heard it said that true patience involves waiting without worrying. Forget all that. Trams stopped running at 1 A.M., and I was worried. Sure enough, the 1 A.M. tram proved to be the last.

At 1:20 A.M. a familiar yellow Sunday School bus pulled to the curb at the opposite corner. Running, waving both hands, I yelled at Elizabeth, who had her head down praying.

While we rejoiced, Brother Hendrix quietly drove us back to the mission home, where we were met by a solemn group of veteran missionaries concerned for our safety.

For the rest of our five-and-a-half-month stay, unless someone experienced went along, I stuck to studying Zulu and helping out through special music and piano lessons. I especially enjoyed opportunities to care for some of the missionaries' kids, and I hated to say good-bye to them when we finally sailed in May for Cape Town.

Of the 41 passengers aboard the Argentine ship *José Menéndez,* seven were missionaries. Argentina being neutral, we sailed under normal conditions except for the small bags of emergency rations each of us carried. While war still raged farther north, we saw no enemy ships and never once glimpsed the telltale snout of a lurking submarine.

The prevailing westerlies were blowing as we sailed through the south temperate zone. Waves pounded the ship at night, making sleep impossible. Peering through the darkness from the door at the end of our passageway, I saw huge waves washing over the second floor deck. Groping, I clung to the banister and crept slowly back to our stateroom.

Voice trembling, I said to Elizabeth, "We need to pray." Around 4 A.M., the ship shuddered violently, then stabilized. The seas gradually subsided, and we were able to sleep.

Breakfast conversation centered around the awful winds and the terrible night we felt fortunate to have lived through. Among the ship's passengers was a shipman en route to Cape Town. He described area weather patterns and explained what had happened.

"We have entered an area where prevailing winds blow with great force. Had the cargo shifted, we could easily have gone down," he told us.

Aware that God had probably awakened friends on the mainland to pray alongside this group of trusting missionaries, we thanked Him for answered prayer.

From Cape Town, as we traveled on by train and bus, we thought of those first Nazarene missionaries to Africa and the 30 grueling days it had taken by mule-drawn wagon to reach our same destination. In 1944 our journey to Swaziland took less than 3 days.

It was raining relentlessly as we stepped off the bus and dashed to a car waiting to take us on up the hill to the large church located at the Bremersdorp (now Manzini) mission station. The church was packed with missionaries and some 400 Swazis, who welcomed us to Africa with a grand reception and with singing we would never forget.

We had been in Swaziland only a short time when I was assigned to work at the Stegi (now Siteki) mission station, teaching part-time in the Bible school and assisting in the dispensary. Plans included living with Ora Lovelace (West). Ora would also be my language teacher.

Language study was difficult for me. No matter how hard I studied, I still made many mistakes. One evening Bessie Tallackson came for dinner. At the end of the meal I said to the cook, *"Kumbula ukudya ikate."*

My guest burst out laughing. "Lorraine," she said, "you just told her to eat the cat!"

We enjoyed a good chuckle together, because I had intended to tell her to *feed* the cat, not eat it. Would I ever conquer this strange Zulu language with the strange "clicks," that causative verb form, and the plurals on the beginning of nouns?

Business conducted at the October 1945 council meeting was much the same as district assembly at home. It was also a time when changes in missionary assignments were often made. World War II had finally ended, and the new recruits had arrived.

"We have a new assignment for you," Field Superintendent W. C. Esselstyn said as this beginner missionary stood with awe before an executive committee made up of veterans. "We would like for you to go to Arthurseat mission station in the Eastern Transvaal [in South Africa] to open a new high school."

My thoughts spun. Why high school and not the Bible college, as I had anticipated? Quickly my heart lifted in prayer. Years prior to this committee's request, before an altar at ENC, I had yielded my all. Now God's Spirit was already saying to me, "Go . . . teach" (Matt. 28:19-20)! With my heart at rest, there could be but one answer.

Faced with a new challenge, I lifted my chin. Peace flooded my soul as I responded quietly, "Yes. I will go."

Glimpses

Dear Father and Mother,

High school opens Wednesday. This is Monday night! It looks as if we will double or triple in attendance this year.

I'm getting more and more excited about my trip home. Won't it be fun on that last lap on the train when I have entered Idaho and know it is only a few hours from home! And you will be excited too! . . . Daddy, please try to take it very easy so when I get home you will be strong.

I love Africa so . . .

Love,
Lorraine

4

Yes, Lord, Yes!

IN JANUARY I PACKED "all my worldly goods" into one crate, two suitcases, and 16 cardboard boxes and moved to Arthurseat mission station near Acornhoek. The work at Arthurseat opened in 1935 and grew rapidly over the next 10 years. Already it boasted a thriving church, primary school, dispensary, and eight outstations. With my help, it would soon have a high school. Carl and Velma Mischke were my welcoming committee. Until Elmer and Mary Schmelzenbach returned from furlough, the old mission house would be my new home.

Built of whitewashed mud brick, its thatched roof leaked so badly that I moved everything into the one room that had a ceiling—only to discover the ceiling also leaked! The fiber rug covering the cement floor was thick and useful and totally unattractive. This was a far cry from my lovely room with Miss Lovelace! As I was trying to decide where to store my books, Rev. Mischke came to my rescue with two nice bookcases he had made from my trunk crates. It being summer, I welcomed the addition of a kerosene-burning refrigerator.

When the time came to open the new high school, only two students showed up for registration. Deeply disappointed after all my preparation, I thanked God for a blessing in disguise after the missionary nurse had to leave because of serious illness. While capable African nurses attended to regular duties, emergencies and major decisions were suddenly up to me. During the nine months we were without an assigned nurse, I arranged work for my students before leaving the classroom and divided my time between school and nursing duties.

While I taught all classes in English, the curriculum was set by the government, and I had to learn methods established by the Transvaal Education Department. Along with basics, Bible classes were required. I added memory work. In chapel, students sang English songs with remarkable rhythm and gusto. Did they know what the words to even their favorites meant?

After explaining so they would not associate the burning of bridges with terrorist activities, I asked them to translate "Every Bridge Is Burned Behind Me" so that its proper meaning could be understood in Shangaan. Here is the best translation into English from their Shangaan:

> *Lo, since I have found my Jesus,*
> > *Knelt low at the Cross one day,*
> *I've left all behind that's sinful,*
> > *Lost my darkness, found the Way.*

Chorus:
Strengthen me, dear Lord, my Savior;
> *Draw me nearer unto Thee.*
I've left everything that hinders;
> *Jesus, I will follow Thee.*

This song has been sung countless hundreds of times over the years and translated into several other African languages.

While my high school students were mostly young men, two married women came faithfully each day, carrying their babies on their backs. I loved visiting in their African homes, and I would often take along used clothing from an effervescent supply sent by Mother. One year her diligence clothed 60 children, enabling them to attend school.

After the Schmelzenbachs returned and I moved into the nurses' vacant cottage with Louise Long and Jessie Rennie, I went with Jessie to see about a patient. Revival meetings were going on, and I fully expected to be back to help with the music and play the folding organ for congregational singing. We walked about 10 miles, attended to the patient, and arrived home around 1 A.M. to find senior missionaries getting ready to send out a search party.

Regardless of my reason for going, home visits provided a way for me to practice Zulu, which I now used for teaching in children's church.

One Sunday as we left the service, 11-year-old Harmon said, "Auntie, do you know what you told us today?" The Schmelzenbachs' children spoke Zulu as well as Afrikaans.

"Tell me," I said.

"You said if we went on in our sins, we would cry 'stars.'"

Once again I had confused two similar Zulu words, one meaning "stars" and the other "tears." However, we were soon to see major changes on the mission station that would make my struggle to speak fluent Zulu insignificant.

Our first answer to prayer came when the mission was able to purchase for a good price the square mile we had been renting, firmly establishing the Church of the Nazarene in the Eastern Transvaal.

Then we turned on lights generated by our very first light plant. A 40-watt bulb seemed brilliant after kerosene lamps. Six months after the lights came on, drillers hit bedrock at 80 feet and discovered a veritable river. Less than a month later, running water had been installed in every home.

Next came the unforgettable Sunday when we all gathered around Elmer Schmelzenbach's radio as Russell V. DeLong's voice came over the airwaves from the United States to Africa for the first time. We cried unashamedly as we listened for 15 minutes to the new *Showers of Blessing* radio program and sang along with songs so familiar to those of us who are called Nazarenes. Besides bringing a little bit of home to missionaries, *Showers of Blessing* became a great evangelistic tool worldwide.

By the time the council met in 1949, Louise Long had been diagnosed with tuberculosis and had gone elsewhere for treatment, leaving me alone to teach school. Still, I expected to be granted furlough.

Following a meeting that lasted well into the night, the executive committee concurred: "We know your father is ill, and your five years have become nearly six. You have our permission to go on furlough. However, we have no one to replace you.

If you decide to go, we have no choice but to close the high school for one year. Please give us your answer in the morning."

I returned to my room that midnight hour to pray. Almost immediately I knew. If a furlough for me meant closing the high school, then I could not go. Many of the students had come from heathen homes. Some had prayed through in church or in chapel and were studying to become teachers, pastors, or pastors' wives. The need for national workers was urgent. As I prayed, God's voice was both loving and clear. My answer would be "I must stay."

With God's help, the decision had been easy. Writing to my parents, who had long anticipated my homecoming, was hard. Then came Mother's reply. "We understand. We would not want you to have to close the school," she wrote, and I felt better.

The new school year opened in January with a record enrollment of 31 in high school, 305 elementary students, and 500 more registered in outstation schools. I began training a young men's quartet.

While the revival that had swept through camps and camp meetings continued and youth camps grew so large we had to make plans to divide, not all was well. Scattered reports of smallpox became epidemic. I had considered it a privilege to assist with the birthing of both African and, occasionally, missionary babies. Now, as thousands received vaccinations and still many died, helping out in the dispensary had turned into a grim ordeal. And while flu would come later, we were all glad when the epidemic ended.

Soon afterward, revival broke out in chapel one morning. Benches became altars, and classes were delayed until 11 A.M. as unsaved students wept and prayed their way to God. When one young lady could not find victory, I went with her to the prayer hut. There she told me she had been dabbling in witchcraft and confessed her sin to God. Elated to know such could be forgiven, she soon knew the peace Christ's presence had given to 10 other students already that morning.

Needing a holiday after a busy school year, I spent two weeks with Mary Cooper in Gazaland, Mozambique, a place I had visited only once but had come to love. To my dismay, a bout with the flu put me in bed for several days, but I was soon well enough to go with Mary to the home of one of her students near the Limpopo River. Delighted over the unexpected visit, our host family killed a goat, which they served for both supper and breakfast, and we spent the night.

Returning to Arthurseat, I could not forget my visit with Mary and how concern tinged her voice as she spoke of the need for trained workers. But a replacement had been found for me, and I could finally have my furlough. I booked passage for December 19 and began sorting and packing in mid-November.

On November 26 I hurried to answer a telephone message at a nearby store and received the sad news that Father had passed away suddenly on Thanksgiving Day. Could I possibly reach home in time for the funeral?

Father's funeral was delayed until after my arrival. In Africa, coworkers had been there to assist me with packing and work through red tape for my flight. At home we were blessed to have friends and church family to comfort us in our bereavement.

I began my deputation work soon after the funeral and spent time with Mother in between. Jane was busy teaching, and my brother-in-law, Oren Vail, helped us with business decisions.

Toward the end of a year that passed quickly, Dr. Esselstyn wrote to say that I had been reassigned to Mozambique to reopen the Bible training school. Having visited Mary Cooper twice at Tavane during my first term, God had already given me a burden for the school. During my five years at Arthurseat, I had learned how to manage school in a tropical country and completed both written and oral exams in Zulu and written exams in Shangaan. My new African language in Mozambique would be Shangaan.

Arthurseat had indeed been a wonderful training school for my future work in Mozambique.

Glimpses

My All

I hear the beat of dusty feet
*   upon the road;*
I see their loss without the Cross,
*   sin's awful load;*
I feel the call, I give my all.
*   Let me go back*
To win the lost, whate'er the cost.
*   I must go back.*

—Lorraine O. Schultz

5

Tongue-Tangled Teacher

LATE CHRISTMAS EVE 1951, I boarded a train bound for New York City and began the first lap of my journey to Mozambique. Portuguese being the official language for that country, I would first go to Portugal for language study, then on to Mozambique for the rest of a seven-year term.

Leaving New York, I found 67 letters, 5 small packets, and 2 telegrams waiting for me aboard the Italian liner *Vulcania*. How wonderful to have friends—and for more than simply warming the heart! Real friends, I knew, would remember me in their prayers.

Broadsided just once by rough weather during our seven-day passage across the Atlantic, we docked at Lisbon, the very port where Columbus landed after his first voyage to the New World.

"There you are!" cried Armand Doll, finally spotting this—as he later put it—"tall, stately lady in the big black hat."

How good it was to see the familiar face of a fellow missionary and to meet Armand's wife, Pauline! We went by taxi to Amoreiras Street (Street of Mulberries) and the boardinghouse where I would live next door to a missionary from a sister denomination.

Right away I began language study with a private teacher. With 45 students in Lisbon for language study that year, I soon learned to grab on to the perpendicular bar on the side of a trolley, search for toe room, and cling for dear life until I reached my destination. Having had leg surgery in the United States before leaving, I found that this was no small accomplishment.

Neither was language study. Evolving from Latin, Portuguese is one of the Romance languages. Softer and less dynamic than the neighboring Spanish language, pronunciation is difficult, especially for Americans with a penchant for speaking in nasal tones.

Throughout that cold winter we pulled on multiple layers of clothing and huddled beside inadequate heaters and tried to study. On sunny days we sometimes found it warmer to study outdoors and try to write with gloves on.

We practiced Portuguese wherever we could, sometimes with unsuspecting shopkeepers eager to make a sale. One day Pauline decided to purchase a handkerchief *(lenço)*. When the shopkeeper suggested she choose from a display of the beautiful and expensive Madeira tablecloths, so popular among tourists, we knew she had used a wrong word—*lençol.*

Invited to attend a small Evangelical church in Lisbon, we found the minister to be a wonderful man of God. He was a great help to us, because he spoke both English and Portuguese. I was sometimes asked to play the organ for the services. To keep me on track, he would stand near the organ and tell me the page numbers in English until I had learned to understand them in Portuguese.

Then came Communion Sunday. As the elements were passed, a holy hush filled the small sanctuary. When all had received the bread and cup and the minister said, "Drink ye all of it," we lifted our glasses and swallowed. Almost in unison, the three of us began to cough and sputter. I looked at Pauline, and we all struggled with laughter.

"I sure hope the Lord will forgive me—this is the first time in my life I ever drank wine," I whispered.

We apologized for our irreverence after the service, and I'm sure the minister forgave us. After that, we tried to be a little more dignified, at least in church. But without laughter and all the tricks we played on each other, we might never have made it through that cold winter and the difficult studies.

The next summer, the Dolls and I went to Coimbra, Portugal, for an intensive six weeks of study at one of Europe's oldest universities. Furloughing British missionaries were kind enough to lend us their apartment. Since there was plenty of room, we lived together and took turns cooking. I knew I had done less than my best the day I burned the toast and came home from class to find it framed and hanging on the wall!

Again, we practiced speaking the language wherever we went. Sometimes after coming home from classes, I leaned out my fifth-floor window and spoke with passersby. During that threefold exercise, I not only practiced my Portuguese but also got to know my neighbors and at the same time avoided trips up and down stairs on my slow-to-heal leg.

When examination day finally arrived, the written test went well. For the oral exam, students stood alone before a black-robed examining board seated across the platform of a large auditorium where classmates made up the audience. Among the last to be called, I found my knees were as melting gelatin when I returned to my seat sometime after 7 P.M. Furtively brushing away tears, I saw Pauline's eyes moisten, and we both put our heads down on our desks and cried.

Faking disgust, Armand said, "I'm taking you two home." Instead, he took us for a nice ride. After supper, Pauline and I went out and had some soothing ice cream.

Despite our fears, we were all awarded certificates in August, marking the end of our first language hurdle. However, we still had to face the Shangaan language spoken in the southern provinces of Mozambique. Portuguese, the official language, was just a beginning.

Assigned to fill in for Lois Drake, I sailed alone for South Africa in December. Though I was excited to be finally returning to Africa, I found it hard to say good-bye to the Dolls, who by now had become my good friends.

In 1952 and again in 1953, we had applied for visas for entering Mozambique. Twice those applications had been rejected. Our third application to

Portuguese authorities had to include the names of the missionaries we would be replacing. Since the Jenkinses were leaving for South Africa, their visa privileges could be given to the Dolls. I would take the place of Bessie Tallackson, who had retired.

As we waited, I spent several months at the Endingeni (now Schmelzenbach Memorial) mission station near Piggs Peak. My ninth grade classroom was in an addition built onto the back of the old stone church built by pioneer missionaries. Along with teaching, I also served as principal and sometimes helped in the dispensary. At the same time I kept on with language study and, to meet requirements, took my Portuguese exams all over again! I also continued pleading with God concerning our visas. For if authorities turned down our third application, the Portuguese government would accept no more requests.

God heard our prayers. After 16 months of waiting, our visas were granted. A telegram arrived the next day from C. S. Jenkins: "PERMITS AT MANJACAZE STOP DOLLS LEAVING TO-MORROW STOP PRAISE THE LORD"

The very next day, I joined the Dolls in Lourenço Marques (later renamed Maputo). From there we would travel the last 200 miles to the mission station together.

"Is it really true?" I asked Pauline.

"Indeed it is," she said. "We are about to enter our Promised Land! God has answered the prayers of His people." While our destination would be more likely to "flow" with mosquitoes, malaria, and heat than with milk and honey, we didn't care. We were on our way.

Early next morning we piled into the Dolls' red Jeep and began our precarious journey to the Tavane mission station. Enchanted with the loveliness of the African morning, we caught glimpses of the beautiful Indian Ocean as we drove our first stretch on paved highway. After the pavement ended, we traveled the next 40 miles on narrow strips of cement barely wide enough for tires.

"What happens if we meet another car?" I asked Armand.

"No problem," he said. "I pull over and drive with one wheel on a strip and the other in the sand. The other driver will do the same."

Heat had settled in by midmorning, and the cement gave way to sandy roads marked by countless detours. We passed small villages filled with African homesteads standing silent beneath a burning sun. We crossed the crocodile-infested Limpopo River by ferry and, an hour later, passed through the edge of Manjacaze village, where we spotted the post office we would appreciate for many years among Manjacaze's few stores and administration buildings.

The last leg of our journey kept us totally involved (without letup!) for a long and tedious hour and a half over an 18-mile stretch of some of the worst road ever. Armand repeatedly shifted into four-wheel drive as the Jeep crawled over rough terrain interspersed with deep pockets of loose sand. Pauline and I wiped perspiration and tried not to complain.

Around 4 P.M. we rounded the last bend and saw several hundred Africans, together with missionaries, lining a driveway strewn with palm branches. Waving palm branches and singing, they directed us to a stopping place. Weariness was forgotten as we were escorted to a small platform and welcomed with speeches and more music. The joyous reception brought a glorious end to our long period of waiting and provided an enthusiastic beginning for our new terms of service. I moved into Mary Cooper's house, a home we were to share for many years.

Four months later, in March 1954, we reopened the Tavane Bible Training School. Recommended by pastors and church boards, 21 students came from churches throughout the three Gaza districts. Some were new converts. But if we were to have workers for tomorrow, it would be necessary for us to train them all.

Along with a language barrier that proved horrendous, there were extreme differences in levels of education. While a fourth grade education was considered good then, only a few could understand Portuguese. Some had learned to read and write—barely—in night school near the gold mines. The rest fell somewhere in between.

Textbooks were unavailable. We had only the Bible, two small booklets in the Shangaan language, and a few mimeographed notes with which to teach. Since I spoke only a little Shangaan at that time, how we got through that first year remains a mystery. For sure, during those first months the teacher learned more than her pupils!

I had used a corner of my veranda that first year for classroom space, but the need for real classrooms was urgent. Slowly enough money came in for a start. Although I had never aspired to a career in carpentry, I suddenly found myself directing a building program. Mary Cooper showed me how to draw the simple plans that were not nearly as complex as for permanent buildings.

"You must use the metric system for measuring," she reminded me. Using my limited knowledge of metrics, I drew plans I hoped would meet with the necessary approval of mission executives. The old wagon we had for hauling supplies seemed always to be in one stage or another of "broken down." On the plus side, God provided us with a carpenter (a Bible school student) and an after-school student work program. Work was plentiful over the next few years as we built classrooms and added substantial huts for housing students.

In 1955 five students graduated from the two-year Bible course. Of these, all three men were later ordained, and the two ladies became district Bible women (teachers). A growing district and the building of new churches increased the need for workers. We added a third-year course in 1956 and a fourth year for theology students in 1957. By November of that same year, seven students had earned fourth-year diplomas. Six of these were later ordained, and the seventh became a district evangelist. Two later became district superintendents.

As we trained workers, we did our best to equip them with a sound knowledge of Scripture and help them find spiritual depth in their individual lives. While the 1957 graduates were all men of spiritual maturity, some of the newer students had never seen a real revival.

Planning revival services in Mozambique has its own unique hindrances. Night services must always take place during a full moon because of lurking poisonous snakes and scorpions. To try to schedule revival following cashew harvest was also futile.

The cashew nut is one of Mozambique's main crops. The fruit, which spoils quickly, is often made into beer. Since few who needed the Lord would be in a condition to attend, beer drinking and revival were not compatible. Still, students steadily came to God in many ways.

A herdboy named Noah Mainga had listened one Sunday morning as Mary Cooper preached beneath a Bimbi tree: "Who is willing to follow Jesus and let Him save you and make you a soul winner?" she asked. Sixteen-year-old Noah accepted the challenge, walked to the front, and became a new creature in Christ.

God spoke to Bessie Tallackson before she retired, and she sent Noah for Portuguese training and to Swaziland's Stegi Bible School for two years, where he was sanctified. Noah then returned home to teach and preach until Leona Youngblood suggested Tavane's theological studies. Noah's response was immediate. "Yes, I would like more Bible training and some theological studies," he said.

Noah graduated in 1957 and was ordained in 1958. That same year, he joined our Bible school staff and served for nearly 18 years as head teacher in the Tavane Bible Training School.

Noah stood tall with the students, teaching as I believe the apostle Paul might have taught. He wept with them at the altar, offered sound advice, and at the same time helped me supervise the building program.

Along with others, Noah's deepest concern was for revival. Consequently, revival came to our school that year—a revival that would spread and multiply. After winds from a nearby tornado ruined our revival tent, we moved to the school and, as revival continued, to the church.

A mighty prayer meeting brought women from their gardens to pray, and testimonies lasted far into the night. Many sought forgiveness; others dedicated their lives or were sanctified. One girl brought her old grandmother to the Lord. The revival produced a bumper crop of spiritually established students who became leaders able to stand during the difficult years ahead.

The next year, my second furlough got me home in time for Christmas, more deputation, and the 1960 General Assembly.

Prior to my 1950 furlough, Alabaster giving had been introduced to the church. Now offerings were being received twice annually from "love" boxes scattered among lay homes and churches. Surely God had inspired a wonderful plan for supplying mission fields with adequate buildings and land.

I could barely contain my thoughts. What if Alabaster funds could one day be used for a new Bible school campus in Mozambique?

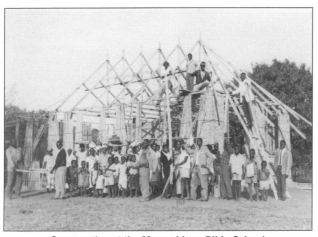

Construction at the Mozambique Bible School

Bible school students and staff

Glimpses

The name Lorraine Schultz will forever be indelibly etched upon the hearts of the people of Mozambique. Our theology gives only a limited place for the doctrine of predestination. However, if we understand the Spirit's probing within the heart of a young girl, then we must say, "Truly Lorraine was predestined by God to be the one to lead the Bible college at Tavane, in the Province of Gaza, at a most strategic moment of history."

Never once did an obstacle to her understood goal of God's will for her life ever appear too large or insurmountable.

Former students lovingly tell anecdotes of the firm hand Professor Schultz placed upon them during their student days. She did not spare herself, and she did not spare her students. The continuing strength of the national church bears the fingerprints of the steady professorial hand of Lorraine Schultz.

The long shadow of a strong-purposed missionary lady continues to point the way to dedicated service, unselfish living, devoted loyalty to Christ and the church, and cherished love for colleagues—missionary and national. That shadow of spiritual reality shall forever pave the way for many to the very gate of heaven.

—Floyd J. Perkins

6

Not Just Peanuts

EXCITEMENT MOUNTED as I looked out over the peanut gardens covering the hill on which the mission station was located. I had returned from furlough just months before, and my dream of building more classrooms was to become reality. Money had come for us to build an Alabaster-funded school. But where? The answer lay before us.

Why not build in the peanut garden?

As the seed of an idea sprouted and grew, the decision was made. We would plant the new Bible school campus on the crest of the hill in the middle of the peanut field less than 500 feet from our house. During the years of moving about and making do with inadequate buildings, we had done our best to make sure students were spiritually grounded. Now we could also claim roots for our building.

Harmon Schmelzenbach III lifted the first shovel of dirt in 1961. By 1970 the completed complex included Jenkins Chapel, seven classrooms, a library, and offices. Built of whitewashed cement block, the buildings' thatched reed roofs formed a thick insulation against Africa's intense heat and held in warmth during the cool season.

In the midst of our building, Vicente Mbanze,

the school's capable music director, expressed a desire for the choir to learn Handel's *Messiah.* Having encouraged the use of good music, I suppose I was partly to blame for what seemed a giant undertaking. He began in April, holding choir practice on weekends and holidays. Following a first presentation in Tavane's Grose Memorial Church, the singing of the *Messiah* became a Christmas tradition. While the music may have lacked some professionally, the harmonious blending of those rich African voices would be hard to surpass.

Harmony between Christian values and African custom also needed to take place in many homes. When some of the women asked for a class to help them in their daily lives, I was stymied.

Almost from the start, we had fed and cared for motherless babies brought to us by family members having no way to feed them. I had gladly supervised the African nurses assigned to this task and had fallen in love with the precious two- and three-year-olds, who had to go back to their families once they could handle solid food. But I had no children of my own. I had never even been married. Respected though I might be concerning biblical and educational matters, I could not ignore African tradition or their beliefs concerning unmarried or childless women.

Then God brought to mind my coworker, Marjorie Stockwell. Married to one husband, Marjorie had known the sorrow of losing a child (a tragedy that happened far too often among our beloved Africans). I knew her children were well behaved, for they had stayed with me many times when

Marjorie needed a rest or travel time with her husband. Marjorie agreed to teach the women, leaving me free for the work I knew best.

During my 22 years as principal and teacher, the school graduated 63 students from the four-year theological course. Another 115 completed the two-year Bible course, and more than 150 others earned either a Christian worker's certificate or completed a one-year course. An alumni association, formed in 1961, continues to offer fellowship and encouragement to graduates and former students.

Having completed most of our new buildings by 1966, I left once more with Doris Brown and Elizabeth Cole for the important business of maintaining connections with the home church. First on the itinerary was a visit to Israel and Jordan. Ralph Earle, a former professor of mine at ENC, had offered to pay additional expenses for a trip intended to enhance my teaching.

Tears filled my eyes on that first day of July as the Royal Jordanian plane dipped low over the airport and I read the word "Jerusalem." Berge and Doris Najarian would be our hosts for the first three days. After we passed through the Mandelbaum Gate into the Jewish section of that still-divided city, Alex and Hallie Wachtel opened wide vistas of learning for me as we visited a variety of new, yet so familiar, biblical sights.

Traveling on to England, we visited John Wesley's home, chapel, and library, and we stood on Aldersgate Street, where Wesley had his "heart-warming" experience. Next came Wales and the site of the great Welsh revival. As we left for home,

I knew I could never be the same after those soul-stretching days steeped with the unforgettableness of my spiritual heritage.

By the time Elizabeth and I had reached America, we had traveled by nearly every means of transportation available. Before my third furlough had ended, I had gone an additional 35,360 miles and enjoyed God's protection every mile of the way. This time my sister, Jane, returned with me to Africa before going on to Australia for a year of sabbatical.

As we drove the 200 miles from Maputo up to the Tavane mission station, Jane asked, "With the hundreds you could work with in the city, why live so far out in the bush? Why such an isolated life?"

"Jane, just wait until you've seen our mission station with all its activities," I said, launching into a detailed description. Simply speaking of our work increased my own excitement, and I hoped Jane would become a little bit excited too.

"Besides the five missionary residences, we've a large church and a day school of more than 400 students," I said. "With the help of six African nurses, our missionary nurses sometimes treat as many as 100 patients a day in our dispensary. This very moment in our Bible school nearly 100 students are in the process of training to become pastors, pastors' wives, and youth workers."

I told Jane that at times we got so busy I was tempted to "take tomorrow to bed" with me. But as I listened next morning to the unique and blessedly familiar "ringing" of African drum "bells" calling us to early prayer, I realized how much better it is to live prayerfully and leave each day's timetable for God to work out.

Following Jane's visit, I settled back into routine, teaching both ancient and church history and theology (my favorites), as well as hygiene and first aid. Knowing that students going out into full-time work must also support their families, we included practical skills such as tailoring and brickmaking whenever possible.

Thinking the subject too advanced even for fourth-year students, when I suggested adding a course in biblical archaeology, my colleagues shook their heads. Convinced that the subject that had so captivated me could help bring Bible history alive, I added it anyhow, and the students loved it. However, as had happened before when I had tried to pass on to students every possible scrap of knowledge that could be crammed into the curriculum, my overloaded boat threatened to capsize. Hearing my distress signal (again!), a patient colleague graciously lifted some of my load and bailed me out.

The evenness of our days was not to last, however, for rumors increased almost daily concerning unrest in the north. Mozambique is but 1,500 miles long. The threat of a Communist takeover was getting too close for comfort. By 1970 conditions had become serious for our mission station in the Tete Province 1,000 miles to the north. Then came a telegram from Oscar Stockwell. Tete Bible School students and their families were being evacuated immediately and would soon arrive at Tavane by special bus.

The cost of food had risen steadily. Even with

our expanded facilities, beds were scarce. How could we possibly care for so many?

When the bus arrived, students rushed from their classrooms, shouting and shedding grateful tears of joy. Sensing the desperate need of the 45 refugees who had endured Communist attack and waited in fear for a split-second rescue that could have come only from God, we tucked them into our hearts and beds and gladly shared rice and mealies.

Regulations tightened as the unrest continued. Burning and looting moved southward. I will never forget what occurred following our own first brief exodus to the safety of South Africa in 1974.

Dusk had started to settle when we arrived back at the mission station. We had heard of the violence that had taken place during our absence. Now we would hear the full story.

As we pulled up in front of my house, there stood Adelina, my cook, and Rosa, who took care of the house. They welcomed me with open arms. I crossed the veranda and went on into the house. In my bedroom I noticed that the cedar chest was missing. I opened a dresser drawer. It was empty. Every drawer, in fact, was empty, as was my clothes closet. In the kitchen, cupboard shelves were bare as Old Mother Hubbard's.

"*Nkosazana,*" said Adelina, using the term for a single missionary. "Don't be alarmed. All of your things are safe."

"We carried them to safety," Rosa explained. "We only waited for your return to bring them back to you."

Glad for the groceries we had purchased before leaving the city, we prepared a meal for the rest of the missionaries, for we were all hungry.

Gradually, we heard what had happened while we were away. On Saturday, September 28, mobs of terrorists had attacked the mission. The evening before, an obviously friendly African had warned our leaders of the planned attack. Bible school students and staff members had worked secretly through the night, carrying my food and belongings to the safety of their own Christian homesteads. Unable to open my cedar chest, they had moved it with its contents undisturbed to a safe hiding place.

My heart melted with love and gratitude. In order to save what belonged to me, my students and fellow teachers had greatly endangered themselves. Had even one African been seen by the enemy, the story would have ended differently. As it was, students carried a little back on their heads each day until drawers and cupboards were again full and all my things back in place. The same happened for others.

Although Mozambique received its independence from Portugal on June 25, 1975, conditions remained unsettled. Missionaries began to evacuate. Pat Buffett and I volunteered to stay and keep the mission going as long as possible. Oscar Stockwell left only after much protest, insisting that two women should not be left alone. But we knew the Communists were scheming for his arrest, and we could not let that happen.

During the weeks we were alone, I often sat down at the piano in the evening, and the two of us would sing. One night as we sang a Bill Gaither song, Pat's voice stopped and then mine as we came to "all fear is gone," because we lived in fear those days. Fear was *not* gone—the living Christ simply enabled us to go on and not be paralyzed by it.

Even though I was determined to hold out against what were rapidly becoming insurmountable odds, when I heard one Sunday from one of our African Christians that the Communist government planned to nationalize unoccupied houses, I ran to get Pat.

"I don't like working on Sunday, but our ox is in the ditch—I think the Lord understands," I said as we lugged food and clothing to Stockwells' partly furnished but deserted home. I then sent word for the district superintendent to bring his family and come sleep in my house, and we did the same with others. If authorities came snooping around on Monday, they would find all houses occupied.

Plagued by repeated Communist attempts to trick us, we hung on and prayed our way through them. One night I heard a car approaching. "It must be Mufundzisi Stockwell!" Rosa exclaimed as it stopped near our kitchen door.

"Surely not this late," I said as together we went to the door. It was dangerous to travel at night.

I could see a woman holding a baby in the car as the driver stepped out. "I am on my way into town, and my petrol is getting low," he said. "Could you sell me a couple of liters? I have money to pay you."

Not knowing if the gasoline was located in the Stockwells' or the nurses' garage, I said, "I'm sure we have petrol, but you'll need to ask Carlos, our truck driver. He will gladly give you some."

"But I have money to pay," he insisted.

Finally, after much argument, he turned and stalked off. I closed and locked the door. Half an hour later, I heard the car drive away.

When Carlos came by early the next morning, I mentioned the incident. Carlos said he had given the man plenty of petrol to get him into town.

Then, "Do you know who that man was?" Carlos asked.

I shook my head.

"He's one of the new government inspectors—the very one who gave us that drum of free government petrol last week. If you had sold him even one drop, he would have let it be known that what the government had given free to the mission, missionaries were now selling in secret to outsiders."

Now, more than ever, any wrong move on our part could be disastrous. Never before or since have I been so glad for a God who does not tire of our much asking.

Then rumor became reality. Armand Doll was arrested.

Glimpses

Jerald D. Johnson tells this story:

Our lives were literally in danger that evening in the city of Maputo in Mozambique. I was there on an official visit, unable to get out because of riots in the streets.

One of the nationals had offered us shelter. We had all the shades pulled. We didn't want anyone to know we were there as we huddled together in the living room, listening to the terrible sounds on the street. One couldn't help but feel the anxiety of these missionaries who had given their lives [to missions], and then to sense how quickly all that could come to an end.

Amid shouts and screams and gunfire, we heard the eerie wail of an ambulance.

At that moment, a voice laced with unshakable optimism echoed across the dim light cast by a single bulb.

"Isn't it wonderful that tonight we have someone here from Kansas City? What a comfort to know, of all the times we might have had a visitor from Headquarters, it is tonight!"

And I was saying to myself, "Lorraine, if you knew how scared I am tonight, you would find no comfort whatsoever in my being here."

7

Escape at Dawn

"PROCEED TO BROOKHOUSE IMMEDIATELY," I read as I clung with shaking hands to a telegram signed by Dr. Coulter and Dr. Johnson.

Ever since Armand Doll had been imprisoned without charge the previous week, Pat Buffett and I had anticipated such a message. While we did not get word until Saturday night, August 30, we learned later that Armand had been arrested on Thursday.

We understood without question the message our leaders were trying to convey. We must leave this land and the people we loved, perhaps never to return.

Noah Mainga had gone to the post office in my car for the telegram that afternoon. "I must waste no time before talking things over with Pat," I thought. Noah drove me to the dispensary.

Returning to the house, I told Adelina we would probably be leaving next morning. Adelina had been my cook for 15 years. She was like family. Pans rattled softly in the kitchen as she prepared our supper. I smelled rice and recognized the rich aroma of chicken and coconut gravy, my favorites.

Hearing her muffled sniffling, I lifted my heart in prayer.

"The song we sang at July's council meeting seems almost prophetic," I said to Pat as we quietly ate our supper. I repeated the words:

In the dark of the midnight
Have I oft hid my face,
While the storm howls above me,
And there's no hiding place.
'Mid the crash of the thunder,
Precious Lord, hear my cry,
"Keep me safe 'til the storm passes by."*
—Mosie Lister

"The storm is certainly howling," I added.

"Yes, but the Lord is also guiding," Pat replied. "He will surely give us the wisdom we need. His promise to me all along has been, 'Though I walk among foes thou dost preserve my life. . . . Thy true love, O LORD, endures for ever'" (Ps. 138:7-8).

"And the promise God gave you—'He will see to it that everything is finished correctly'—is not just for you. The dispensary is in its best condition ever to be turned over to our African nurses."

Since travel would be safer by daylight, we decided to pack what little we could take in my Volkswagen Beetle and plan to be on the road by 6 A.M. We would leave behind some 10,000 Nazarenes. God, we believed, would preserve our work.

After we had eaten, Pat met with her nurses, and I joined my Bible school staff in their prayer meeting to explain the situation. As I left them and tramped through sand to the hut of one of the Bible women to say a hasty good-bye, the great silence of Africa seemed to surround me. How I loved every foot of that campus, where so many spiritual battles had been fought and won!

O God, I prayed, *keep Thy hand upon this Thy work and upon those who have studied here and prepared themselves to go forth and proclaim Thy Word.*

The night lay blanketed in impenetrable darkness. Using my flashlight at intervals, I quickly walked down the path toward home and began the dreaded task of deciding what to take and what to leave behind. My books—a collection of 40 years—would mostly have to stay. Finally I settled on a few necessities. By 1 A.M. my suitcase was ready.

I called Adelina and Rosa, and we slipped quietly out of the house to load the car. Gripped by strange tension, we could only watch and pray that the usual spying soldiers slept soundly and were not on patrol. I could see Pat's light still burning in her house; so the girls went down the path and brought up her cases. Thinking ahead to our journey's needs, I hid money throughout the car to be used for food or gasoline in case of emergency. Inside, I extinguished the Aladdin lamp beside my bed, lay down, and quietly began to pray.

An hour later, the alarm jangled. It was still dark. As dawn tinged the eastern skyline, I could hear Adelina moving about in the kitchen. I knew her heart was heavy as she prepared a bountiful breakfast for us.

During the night, Noah had dug up the emergency money I had buried months before. We were far from a bank. He would hide it in a safer place to be used for continuing the Bible school work until the end of the semester. Together we talked over the housing situation and the mission work in general. I can still hear District Superintendent Benjamin Langa's last few words to me:

"Please come back as soon as you can."

On Wednesday morning, September 3, we hastily gathered the last few items and hurried to the car. Noah would accompany us and help drive. Since we had not told the church people we were leaving, only about 20 came to see us off—the pastor and Bible women, our Bible school staff, the nurses, and, of course, our house help. The pastor led us in quiet song, then Benjamin Langa prayed. Our hearts nearly burst as Noah slid beneath the wheel. When would we ever return?

As the little green Beetle pulled slowly away, some waved, while others could only brush away tears. Soon we had crossed the mission boundaries and were passing the manioc gardens. Sandpipers, hammerkops, and other birds flew out of our path.

An hour later, we had left the remote area and entered the small town of Manjacaze. We had traveled only a short distance from town when we encountered our first roadblock. Frelimo soldiers surrounded the car. Would they search us?

Noah leaned out and spoke a few words. They waved us on. By 10 A.M. we were in Xai-Xai. Here we broke our journey, taking time out for cold drinks, for the day was hot. Two hours later we paused for a quick lunch.

By 1 P.M. we had reached Maputo and were headed across the city to the home of Hugh Friberg. Hugh and Evelyn had been with us for only two councils. Already we had come to love and appreciate these busy pastors of First Portuguese Church.

We pulled beneath their apartment house portico. Pat got out and pressed the buzzer. I could hear Evelyn's voice on the intercom, asking what was wanted.

Recognizing Pat's voice, she called, "Come right up!"

Evelyn met us at the head of the stairs, both children clinging to her skirts. But where was Hugh?

Displaying little of the fear she must surely have been experiencing, Evelyn explained, "Hugh is in prison. He was taken the night after Armand's arrest. There is no charge on either of them."

"You mean Hugh has been in for five days and we've not known?"

"Another message just came for you." She unfolded a tiny scrap of paper.

"If they [Pat and Lorraine] come," it read, "you'd better all go quickly without waiting around, for I fear they'd be held for questioning."

The frightening words spurred a quick decision.

The Fribergs' station wagon was at one of the neighbors' and had not been nationalized. Since it was considerably larger than my VW, Pat and Evelyn went after it. We transferred the baggage and loaded Evelyn's hastily packed suitcases into the back.

I walked over to Noah, whose face was sorrowful. "Noah," I said in a voice that quavered, "if we do not return, my car will be yours. Take it back to the mission and use it there. Please explain our sudden departure to the students and our church friends. We will be praying for you. You have been a great blessing to me these many years."

We climbed into the Fribergs' car and slowly pulled away from the portico. But how does one get a car across an international border (from Mozambique into South Africa) with its owner in prison and his wife without a driver's license? It cannot be done.

But God!

Three months before, four-year-old Gayla Friberg had needed to go to South Africa for a dental appointment. Hugh was busy that day, and Pat happened to be in Maputo waiting for repairs on her car. She volunteered to take Evelyn and the children to South Africa in the Fribergs' car. Relieved to have the problem so easily solved, Hugh had filled out papers showing Pat as the car's driver and had them notarized. Those papers were still valid!

Pat cautiously maneuvered the car out into the beautifully shaded street and turned right. Off to the left we could see the top of the prison that held our "Paul and Silas." What must Evelyn be thinking as we left her husband behind?

Moving into the traffic, we passed red-roofed homes and boardinghouses, places of business and pavement cafés. Soldiers were everywhere as we drove on toward the outskirts of the city and turned north onto the road leading to the South

African border. The children bounced excitedly, obviously enjoying the unexpected trip far more than their mother and "aunties." Anxiously comparing watches, we let the children bounce. Already it was 4 P.M., and we had to reach the border before night!

With roads paved clear to the border post 75 miles away, we made good time. Leaving the shimmering Delagoa Bay, we headed for the small town of Boane, crossed the Umbeluzi River, and continued on through isolated countryside until we were stopped near Ressano Garcia on the border by a second roadblock.

The Frelimo soldiers appeared friendly as they asked to search our car. We climbed out and waited. The inspection slowly continued. Twice we watched nervously as a small plane circled overhead. At last the soldiers waved us on. We would meet our final hurdle at the border post just ahead. Were all our papers in order?

At the border post we filed silently into the customs building. After filling out exit papers, we handed over our passports to be stamped with *saida* (exit) permits to leave the country. I searched my purse. Where, oh, where was that permit? Pat calmly located it.

Finally, at 6:30 P.M., all was in order. Given permission to leave, we sank into our car seats and watched as guards raised the iron gates for us to pass through. As those gates closed behind us and we started toward the South African side of the border, we were overwhelmed with deep gratitude. Like the children of Israel, our Red Sea was behind us. So were those who would harm us. Armand and Hugh, however, were still in prison.

Later that night a South African radio station broadcasting from Johannesburg announced, "Three missionaries and two children have just crossed the border safely."

Glimpses

Manjacaze
August 3, 1977

Greetings from us here at Tavane.

Last week we church leaders crossed the blackest time in history of the church in Gaza.

Authorities came on Monday. We were shamefully condemned, expelled from the missionary residences, and accused as reactionaries, thieves, and antirevolutionaries.

Bible teaching was forever banned. . . . Religion was to be stamped out. Keys confiscated . . . and the Land Rover. [We were] told to remove all religious books from every house. All mission property seized except the church.

On Thursday five families had to go out from the mission houses. . . . Our last home was in the House of the Lord, the Tavane church building.

But then the Lord intervened. . . . Our enemies are dumbstruck.

8

Safe—
but Grounded

WE WERE SAFE IN SOUTH AFRICA. Mrs. June Alexander, missionary president of the South African European District, wrote on their missionary page, "During the past few weeks we have experienced afresh the challenges and responsibility of being a part of the family of God. What a volume of prayer has ascended to the throne of grace on behalf of our missionaries in Mozambique! Many of the missionaries have lost practically all their earthly belongings after having given 22 years of service to that country."

Some of us moved up to the missionary holiday home in Pretoria-Brookhouse to recuperate from the trauma we had experienced over so many stress-filled weeks. On October 27, George Coulter, general superintendent, and Jerald Johnson, then director of the Department of World Missions, met with us in Johannesburg. Virginia Benedict, Pat Buffett, and I were granted early furloughs, with the hope that within a year the turmoil in Mozambique would have come to an end.

To rush home, plunge directly into deputation,

and be asked repeatedly to speak of all we had been through was not what I wanted to do. After voicing my concerns to Dr. Coulter and Dr. Johnson, I asked, "May I return to the States via Israel and do my resting there?"

Dr. Johnson smiled. "Might not that be jumping from the frying pan into the fire?"

I pled my case. "Things seem fairly quiet now. And there is much to be learned in Israel—facts to enhance my Bible teaching—inspiration."

The two men conferred briefly, explained that I must pay any additional expenses, and granted my request. Then Dr. Johnson promptly took care of some of that expense by contacting the Najarians, who arranged for me to stay for a month in their church guest room in Jerusalem.

As I took notes and learned things that would be of help to me for years to come, the trauma eased. Rested and renewed, carrying less luggage than I had ever traveled with before, I then returned to the United States via England to begin another busy year of deputation. The flight to safety had taught me that enough suitcases may still be too many. From then on I traveled so lightly I considered it a compliment when one pastor asked, "Is that all the baggage you carry?"

The year 1976 was one of adjustment and concern. Our hearts were with our Nazarene "Paul and Silas," still confined in the prison camp. Bits of news came in a variety of ways from our beloved Africans in Mozambique:

"We have had much rain, like in 1917. This year it rained from December 4, 1975, until May 29,

1976. The floods have been terrible, and now there is great famine. Your car, the Volkswagen Beetle, has been taken by the authorities. People are suffering! No medicine, no rice, no corn, no peanuts, no sugar, and no salt. Concentration camps have been set up. We need your prayers. But the church continues, sometimes under trees."

How we thanked God for the few positive messages that came through!

That spring my deputation tour took me to beautiful British Columbia, with its majestic mountains and unsurpassed scenery. As I listened to those friendly Canadian Nazarenes pray for Mozambique, my heart was warmed by their concern.

One day as I was in Oliver, British Columbia, having dinner with Kenneth and Ann Stark, former missionaries to Swaziland, the phone rang.

"It's for you, Lorraine," Dr. Stark said.

Wondering who had caught up with me clear across the border, I quickly recognized Dr. Johnson's voice.

"We have exciting news for you," he said. "Hugh Friberg is being released from prison. He'll be home in a few days." Our prayers were being answered!

My next stop being Vancouver, God's timing for me was again perfect. I would be in Vancouver for the grand reunion.

A large crowd filled the waiting area in Vancouver's air terminal that day, including Hugh's parents, Rev. and Mrs. Raymond Friberg, who lived nearby. Tears dripped onto the front of my dress as

Hugh and Evelyn stepped off the plane and Hugh saw his children for the first time in eight months.

When little Mike proudly and unabashedly announced to a waitress, "My daddy's been in prison, you know," the innocent revelation marked another answer to prayer. Throughout all they had been through, God had miraculously protected the children from trauma. Now we needed to trust Him for still one more answer.

Everywhere I spoke over the next few months, I urged churches to pray without ceasing for Armand Doll's release and for our people in Mozambique. One Saturday afternoon as I stepped off a Greyhound bus in Philadelphia, I heard happy voices and sensed excitement among those who had gathered to meet me.

"Armand Doll has been freed—he's on his way to New York!" someone called out.

Heart pounding, I begged my host to please find me a telephone so I could call Pauline.

"It's true!" Pauline shouted into the phone. "God has answered prayer! Dr. Johnson got word yesterday. Armand's plane arrives late tomorrow afternoon. I leave for New York in the morning."

How difficult those 13 months must have been for Pauline! Now her waiting was over. I thanked God for a praying church.

When friends offered to take me to the airport following the morning service for the big welcome, I struggled with temptation. As much as I wanted to be there, the pastor was sick. I could not abandon the evening service.

God wiped away my disappointment through

a single announcement. There would be a welcoming service for Armand on Monday night. And then He blessed my ministry. Next day, District Superintendent Paul Mangum and his wife, Jerri, drove me to that wonderful service of praise and welcome.

As the year of deputation came to an end, my heart was heavy. The door to return to Mozambique had closed. While I had not been well, I had assumed as God's will a reappointment to serve as girls' matron and teach in the Bible college in the Portuguese-speaking country of Brazil. So I applied for my visa.

My illness continued. Then the visa was delayed. After consulting with my physician, Robert Mangum, and with Jerald Johnson, I reluctantly agreed that, at 62, I would retire. This most difficult of all the decisions I had ever had to make proved both wise and timely. Four months later I entered the hospital in Nampa, Idaho, for major surgery— not in Brazil, where my physical needs could so easily have been a liability to myself and to others.

As it turned out, God had great plans for me that would bring harm to no one and would "give [me] hope and a future" (Jer. 29:11, NIV).

Glimpses

Some of Lorraine's friends and neighbors at Casa Robles reflect on her time there:

"Who but Lorraine could persuade us all to help her? You'd offer to help plan for a missionary's visit and find you'd agreed to make the cake, serve the tea, and have them for dinner."

"We were visiting her [Lorraine's] Casa Robles cottage for the very first time. Lorraine slipped a cola can with plastic spill beside Phil's chair. Phil bumped it and was horrified. Lorraine bubbled with delight."

"As we left the convention, the pink traffic ticket tucked beneath the windshield wiper on Casa Robles' van looked real indeed. It was a hoax. The culprit? Lorraine, of course!"

9

Dig This Retirement

I FELT AS IF MY MISSIONARY WINGS had been clipped. Following recuperation from my surgery, I flew to Los Angeles and a cottage reserved for me at Casa Robles, our Nazarene missionary retirement center in Temple City, near Pasadena, California. The Dolls happened to be visiting at Casa Robles. To my surprise, they were at the airport to greet me.

"What blessed provision the church has made for retired missionaries!" I thought as we entered the landscaped campus in the San Gabriel Valley, 15 miles northeast of Los Angeles. Stately palms flanked the front steps of Sanner House, the main building. Soon after moving into No. 18 of Casa Robles' 32 cottages in May 1977, I discovered my neighbors had all come from worldwide and often exotic addresses, including Africa.

During that first year of recuperation and adjustment, I came to love this new family of retired missionaries. Since I was feeling much better physically, when an old friend handed me a brochure and told me about a biblical archaeology tour to Israel, seminar included, I decided to go. The next year friends offered funds for a Bible lands study in Greece, Egypt, Jordan, and Israel. I couldn't miss that, of course.

A few weeks before I was to leave for Israel, I received a letter from Hugh Friberg, who had been reappointed to South Africa.

"We hear you are going to the Middle East," he wrote. "Could you consider coming on from there to help with literature work and make it possible for Rose Handloser to furlough? We would be glad if you could phone us."

Africa, land of my calling, where I had spent 33 years! God could perform another miracle for the needed finances. My hand shook as I dialed direct. Hugh answered immediately.

"Your letter came this morning! When do you need me?" I asked. Overjoyed, Hugh explained the urgent need for someone to prepare NWMS, Sunday School, and other materials for six months. I had taken the step of faith, and God had given the green light. Now for the miracle.

One morning a plain, small envelope arrived in the mail. Out dropped a check for $1,500 and a brief note from an old friend: "The enclosed is from the estate of my sister. She loved you dearly." Rushing out of the house, I hurried down the drive to Louise Chapman's cottage to share the wonderful news with her.

I repeatedly thanked God during an incredible year overseas. Following the seminar in Israel, I moved into the parsonage at Nazareth while Merlin and Alice Hunter enjoyed a short furlough. After preaching through an interpreter on Sundays, I taught Christian life training classes and did other tasks through the week. Sometimes I went on Mondays to Earl and Norma Morgan's in Jerusalem, and we drove the six miles to Bethlehem for more Christian life classes.

Bethlehem is in hill country, its star-studded nights clear and crisp. How we welcomed visiting in those homes over a cup of Middle East black coffee at the end of those sessions. Sometimes I felt like pinching myself; I would think, "Nazareth! Bethlehem! Jerusalem! If this is retirement, I love it!"

My beloved Africa came next. I boarded a plane in Tel Aviv and flew to Johannesburg for a busy six months in the literature office. In addition to preparing Sunday School lessons to be translated into several of South Africa's Bantu languages, I wrote other literature.

When the year ended, I took time to audit a class at the Institute of Holy Land Studies on Mount Zion during a stopover in Jerusalem on my way home. Occupied at times by furloughing missionaries, my cottage at Casa Robles was waiting for me. It was indeed a "haven of rest." It was home.

Home, it turned out, was a good place to be. After my surgeon recommended open-heart surgery in 1983, I soon found myself in Huntington Memorial Hospital in Pasadena, recuperating from four bypasses. Thanks to the prayers of friends and my church, the surgery went well. Nine months later, I was ready for another seminar in Israel that included a short dig near Tel Aviv.

Under the direction of archaeologists Amahai Mazar and Roy Blizzard, our team began digging in Roman levels, dealing with artifacts from both Old and New Testament times. We excavated a plastered cistern from the late Roman period, unearthed a beautifully preserved Roman vase, and swept off the balks and walls of an already excavated Philistine temple.

From that dig on, my immediate future was in ruins—ruins of cities in Bible lands, that is, for many developments came out of these studies:

1. Forty articles, published in assorted Sunday School quarterlies.

2. The Los Angeles chapter of the Biblical Archaeology Society, founded in my Casa Robles cottage, which has for 15 years provided programs led by outstanding archaeologists from California and Israel throughout the community.

3. Hundreds of photographs of ancient biblical sites published in textbooks and magazines.

4. Fifteen years of participation in biblical archaeology seminars held during NIROGAs (Nazarene International Retreat[s] Of Golden Agers).

5. A series of books on biblical archaeology for teens, teamed with my archaeology friend Babs Miley. My two: *Discovering Jerusalem* and *Discovering the New Testament.*

6. A textbook in Portuguese for the Mozambique Bible school, *Old Ruins Still Speak Today,* to be used on our Portuguese-speaking mission fields.

Soon after going to Casa Robles, acting on the admonition of Dr. Johnson, I began to improve my writing skills through writers' conferences and the

Christian Writers' Guild. As I wrote missionary reading books (*Mozambique Milestones, Casa Robles: House of Oaks, Because Someone Prayed,* and *Bringing God's Word to Guatemala*), reading books for children, and all those other mailings, I must have driven Charles and Roma Gates crazy with my constant popping in to use the office fax machine or photocopier. If I could just once have remembered that Monday was their day off!

Through good news and bad, I had continued to correspond over the years with some of my former students in Mozambique. We rejoiced with them and experienced heart heaviness. Then, early in the 1990s, the long period of unrest began to wane. The David Restrick family moved to Mozambique, and David became academic dean of the seminary. While it seemed unlikely that I should ever join them, I could pray and send parcels or gather funds, which I did from time to time.

Then I heard that my church for 17 years in Temple City was sending a Work and Witness team to Mozambique. An unimagined dream came true when they gave me a ticket to go with them. (Thank you again, Pastor Ronald Kearns and team!)

En route for London, British Airways flight 282 soared into the air from Los Angeles on June 25, 1993. Aboard were one Work and Witness team; its director, Clell Barker; and one retired missionary who could barely contain her excitement. I knew I could not lay bricks for the new Polana Church like the other 14, but even after 18 years of absence, I could still witness in the language of its people.

As we crossed the border from Swaziland into

Mozambique, our minds were etched with reminders of a senseless war. We passed the burned-out wrecks of 80 cars and trucks along a road where 2,500 people had lost their lives. Then we saw the far-distant harbor and the sparkling Indian Ocean and drove on toward the high-rise buildings marking the skyline above the capital city, where we were to erect a new church building.

Early next morning our team began work at the building site. Surely, in a city of nearly 1.5 million, supplies could be easily found. Not so. While most of the material was already in hand, prayer, patience, and a veritable miracle or two had to take place before David Restrick was able to gather up the last few items.

African Nazarenes provided the daily noon meal of fish or chicken, cornmeal porridge, and rice for our team of volunteer bricklayers. Mrs. Restrick and Heather Howie worked with team members through the day to prepare our evening meal. A shortage of water hindered both cooking and clothes washing. On Saturday at the dedication service, the team presented the pastor with a beautiful hand-carved pulpit. The next day I was privileged to preach in the larger city church to nearly 2,000 people, and the altar was lined with seekers. If I had to leave Africa once more, what a blessed way to go!

Like Work and Witness teams across the country, our people returned to Temple City and their regular jobs and homes. But they would never be the same. For this loving, giving method of service has brought great blessing to churches and team members as well as to missionaries and the people they serve throughout the world.

Unlike the many who could choose to go again, my opportunity to travel for Work and Witness soon became but a cherished memory. I had to make another change.

Lorraine "on the job" with the 1993 Work and Witness team

Glimpses

"We must plan for a writing seminar—this fall," Lorraine said. "We must get organized." (She was working on this book at the time.) But writers would rather write than plan, and aspiring writers prefer to be led. Who would do the planning?

"I will, then," said the little red hen (Lorraine). And so she did!

She asked God for 50.

Sixty-one came.

10

Full Circle

BACK AT CASA ROBLES following the Work and Witness trip, I faced a new problem. "Mr. Arthur Itis," the harasser who had become such a bother to some of my friends, had moved in alongside my growing list of ailments. After discussing alternatives with my Lord, I made an appointment with Jane Tustin, our Casa Robles nurse. In 1960 we had traveled to Africa together by freighter; she had been my nurse for 14 years.

Jane had been there for bypass surgery and monitored medication for my ailing heart. When a diabetic condition interfered with healing, she had been the one to tenderly bathe and wrap my feet and watch carefully over me for days on end in her own home. Jane was also the friend who helped me order my special shoes. I could trust her advice.

"I don't want to leave Casa Robles," I said, "but you know how I've been struggling with arthritis."

She nodded. "I know. Lots of pain. Well, you *are* going on 80."

"Perhaps it's time to consider a place with fuller retirement," I said.

"Some of our missionaries have found the

Episcopal Home in Alhambra quite comfortable," Jane suggested.

"My sister wants me to go back to Nampa, Idaho, where I'll be closer to family."

"Jane?"

"Yes, her name is the same as yours."

My nurse also knew about the tablespoon of pills prescribed for daily maintenance. I said, "Maybe prices will be more reasonable in Idaho. I hope so. The cost of prescriptions has gotten so high, my doctor may soon have to say, 'Take one pill as often as you can afford it.'"

Deciding to leave Casa Robles was not easy. I would miss the beautiful campus with its graceful palms and sunlight filtering through the branches of the great California live oaks. Thursday mornings, when we gathered in the Sanner House living room to pray for world missions, had been a blessing. I would miss Biblical Archaeology Society meetings and the Temple City Historical Society, where I was a charter member. Then there was the Sunday School class I taught at Temple City Church, all my friends, and my next-door neighbor, Betty Sedat. We had done so many wonderful things together.

On the plus side, during the months it took for me to decide, my sister, Jane, and her husband had left Canada to also retire in Nampa near family. After the long years of separation, it would be nice to have them close by. Besides, I had prayed much about the matter. To apply for regular retirement at Sunny Ridge Manor Retirement Center in Nampa seemed the right thing to do.

My decision made, I was faced with the hectic business of downsizing furnishings from a four-room house to fit into one room. Bit by bit, I sorted out necessities. This time my beloved books could go with me. Friends helped me with a yard sale to dispose of the rest. I said my good-byes, then Charles and Roma Gates, Casa Robles' delightful directors, drove me to the airport.

I loved Sunny Ridge Manor from the beginning. With my sister living just two blocks away, and NNC, my alma mater, about one mile, I soon felt at home. Many old friends were also enjoying their retirement years at Sunny Ridge, and this meant added blessing.

For the gala occasion of my 80th birthday, I invited six guests. Used to keeping occupied, I arranged right away to speak in faith promise services and missionary chapter meetings. When the chaplain told me he could use a substitute, the additional opportunity to speak for my Lord brought joy to a life already brimmed with God's goodness.

For 50 years I had been a member of the Michigan District. Now it was time to return to the church that had welcomed me to the West during college days and supported my missionary efforts with prayer and in other ways for so many years. On September 24, 1995, Pastor Daniel Ketchum again welcomed me into membership at Nampa College Church. I soon discovered that my old/new church was a strong missionary church. And I thanked God that it was also a praying church.

In my new home I found time to look into the past. As I reread some of the 200 or more letters I had received from former students, I saw how faithfully God had blessed our work in Africa. While reading a letter written in 1986 by Jonas Mulate, remembering his struggles before an altar of prayer as a student, I rejoiced once more over his words:

"I am very happy to write you this letter today. I'm still in God's ministry and am preaching the Word. Since 1982, I have served the church full-time. This is the fruit of you and other missionaries who are retired." The letter was signed, "Your respectful son, Jonas Mulate."

Another letter in 1990 said that Jonas had moved with his family to the north part of Mozambique, to Nampula, home of the largest unreached tribe in all of Africa, perhaps in all the world. Within eight months, 700 were added to the church. Eight promising young people were sent south to attend Bible college. By 1995 the number of Nazarenes in northern Mozambique had grown to 9,154. Buildings are presently being completed on a new campus for the Nazarene seminary of Mozambique, with Simeon Mandlate, another former student, as director.

During these, my retirement years, each time I receive such reports, I think my blood pressure goes up. I thank God for rapid and worldwide communication that helps us know quickly how to pray.

These days with my physical limitations, other than filling in for our chaplain, scheduling chapel programs, substituting for my Sunday School teacher, judging poetry contests, sending parcels to Mozambique, entertaining missionaries, keeping up with Jane's children and grandchildren, or writing letters and occasional articles (and now this book), praying is about all I can do.

Still I am content.

For "I have fought a good fight, I have finished my course, I have kept the faith: henceforth there is laid up for me a crown of righteousness, which the Lord, the righteous judge, shall give me at that day: and not to me only, but unto all them also that love his appearing" (2 Tim. 4:7-8, KJV).

Epilogue

Betty Sedat remembers:

Lorraine Schultz's life to me is like a book on life's bookshelf. Before this book closed for the last time, I wanted to say good-bye. The trip was a kind of pilgrimage.

The memorial service for Lorraine was a beautiful service in College Church [Nampa] with about 200 attending. As a part of the pilgrimage, I went to see her room in the retirement home. Then on to the medical unit to visit the little room where she had slipped away to be with her Lord. Following an evening of looking at photos, I said, "This is enough. Lorraine is a beautiful memory."

But when you've read a good book or story, the aroma lingers on. She was my next-door neighbor at Casa Robles. I learned to love her and was flabbergasted at the multitude of her accomplishments. Hands and mind were incessantly busy, often until 1 A.M. She was always making plans for the future, "booking" for this tour or that event. I was often amused that she was never at a loss to ask for things like yarn for Mozambique or other items. When she got ready to go to Nampa, she had everybody scurrying around.

But as my eye travels down life's bookshelf, I see some big and important books. These will never be closed—at least not before Christ returns.

Here's one titled Africa. I open it and find many pages are about Lorraine Schultz.

I read of how she returned to Mozambique and over 100 of her former students came to greet her and thank her for teaching them spiritual truths and practical values. Even after Lorraine's retirement, she continued loving and tirelessly doing for them. This impressed me deeply. Her influence in Africa will go on and on.

And more and more pages will be added to that Africa book.